SEEDS

UNDER

THE

TONGUE

ECOPOETRY

SEEDS

UNDER

THE

TONGUE

ECOPOETRY

TIMOTHY P. MCLAUGHLIN

Homebound Publications
Ensuring that the mainstream isn't the only stream.

HOMEBOUND PUBLICATIONS
Ensuring the mainstream isn't the only stream
Postal Box 1442, Pawcatuck, Connecticut 06379-1442
WWW.HOMEBOUNDPUBLICATIONS.COM

Quantity sales. Special discounts are available on quantity purchases
by corporations, associations, bookstores and others. For details, contact
the publisher or visit wholesalers such as Ingram or Baker & Taylor.

Published in 2019 ♦ Homebound Publications
Front Cover Image © Freestocks.org
Cover and Interior Designed by Leslie M. Browning
ISBN ♦ 978-1-947003-54-5
First Edition Trade Paperback

10 9 8 7 6 5 4 3 2 1

Homebound Publications is committed to ecological stewardship.
We greatly value the natural environment and invest in environmental conservation.

Rooted & Risen

for love of earth & the earthly

especially my enchantress Madi
and our brood of three wild-bodied, beautifully-voiced creatures:
Anjamora, Tadhg, Fiadh

~

CONTENTS

Only These, And This

ALLIES

ENCOUNTERS

CHURCH

ANCIENTS

ROOT

"...did [Cormac mac Airt] one day come thunderstruck down from the hills, wild nature and druidic culture singing a perfectly single song in him?"

–JOHN MORIARTY, *Invoking Ireland*

ONLY THESE, AND THIS

The animal of me, as it turns out,
requires very few things:

> a jug to hold water,
> a pit to tend fire in,
> a stone to dig down with,
> the ongoing garden of the wild,

>> sun on the eyes, air in the chest,
>> the passage of clouds overhead,
>> a soft place to lie dreaming,
>> and a voice to tell you what I've seen.

Give me these, again and again,
spread anew on the altar of daybreak

> and I will make stories
> out of the clear sounds I've heard
> and the brief enchantments I've felt,

>> my breath perchance coming into
>> a usefulness that some beloved son
>> or fine daughter may feed on,
>> long after it expires, like starlight;

or else go unnoticed,
a lone candle burning faithfully

> in a round room, gathering
> every intensity, until its light
> is snuffed and consumed

>> by a pervasive darkness
>> that awaits my silent homecoming
>> with perfect indifference.

ALLIES

TREE SPEAK

Everything changed when I began to speak to
the trees rather than of them. Began to know

them as near kin as well as distinct Others. Felt
a full-bodied yearning to be close, very close to

them awaken in me. And found—what else!—that
they yearn back for me, and they too speak. In the

leaves or needles most readily, low-lit or snow-laden
or wind-dancing, but in ways beyond too. For when

I reach out my palm toward that rough-barked skin,
the tree nearly leans in to the touch and pulls my

forehead close to its sturdy body. And standing thus
embraced, the speaking deepens as the roots' marriage

to the soil whistles faintly in my ears. Then, entranced,
the rapid gulping or slow breathing of this being sounds

startlingly through my skull. And when I upturn
my face to behold the full display of those untiring arms

splayed in the delicate airspace above, I must respond:
an exuberant series of whoops quickslips from

my throat and resounds over the hills. No word or
string of them could say what is moving through me

now. And the tree, I sense, becomes likewise elated
by the exchange. The warmed mood between us is so

inviting, I feel I can ask anything, and I have. If I
should marry; or carry an altar; or vanish for a time;

if a baby would come, and come again; and if my tongue
should sing poems, if the Earth needs this or another,

lighter food. And I've become bold enough to inquire of
these tall ones if they are really well, how deep and

irreversible the sicknesses are among them, and in the fresh
waters and dark soils; and if the stars still have medicine

to doctor it all. Maybe it helps, my speaking thus to these
long standing friends. To them, we surely are like children,

careless and little aware what is tended for us by them, our
elders, who tend on even when we messily reverse their work

and take and take often without a moment's contemplation
or a humble asking and likely without the listening,

and then, somehow, the dreamy conversing I have come
to love beyond compare and now could not do without.

ROADRUNNER

Meeting you in the high desert was like the
day my wife first stepped into my gaze: happily
blinded by a sudden mysterious comfort flooding
the eyes like sunrise. Somehow, among all the kings of
skies I've courted and all the lords of hills I've knelt
to, you are my rightful match, my own slender likeness
poured into a winged mold. You once came boldly to
my mud hut and called me out—a clear, curious warble
all its own—then stood in full regalia: your royal neck
erect, your spiked headdress fluffed up, your black,
white-tipped tail feathers fanned out fluently, your lean
thoroughbred legs at ease. I was dizzy in the thrill of
your presence—like an apparition—and you gave me
your eye for a wondrous instant, then leapt off the
hillside in a swift floating dive and scuttered into the
sticks and shadows. On an ordinary morning turned
remarkable, I found one of your tribe along my running
trail, laid out in death's long dream. I scooped up the
feathery mass and brought it home, awed to touch those
elusive speedy claws and that signature hair puff.
I plucked and washed the feathers and discovered in some
a subtle green warmth glowing within the dark hues and
knew their medicine was deep and good. My beloved
formed those feathers as a fan that I hold aloft when I dance
before the tree of life to open summer's shades. Each time
I unwrap the coverings of that fan, I feel into your truth and

thereby mine and supplicate you again, noble ally: Teach me
fleetness in my ways; Bring me elegance in my movements;
Help me know how and when to run out open, or float
up easy, or hide away certain, or stand to be seen in my
feathers and claws and heard in a voice unlike any other.

EAGLE DANCE

Surrendered to the mountain's steady hold,
I lie flat in a savored pause at the farthest
point out on the day's walk. You enter in
a blink, as if conceived anew from the great
blue dome. Your appearance—two of you
black-feathered bodies in near orbit—draws
the creature me into a heightened presence,
a rapt attention, not wanting to miss a moment
of your dance…Whenever I've been witness
to your twirling atop the zenith, everything
stops. Always the choreography is distinct
and riveting. And always you turn up when
I most require it, as I teeter on the edge of
the typical hopelessness and palm the soggy
fruit of another well-imagined despair.
And where is that sorrow really? your circling
and rising speaks to me, *Launch yourself up
here and vision things through our wider,
wilder lens. Flip & dip & spin round wide to
the bright center point we've printed in the sky this
instant, already fading into a new Now as we motor
out & out & disappear into the big Empty, still
loving you, lovely one, but clutching nothing at all.*

BEAR TALK

I have smelt long into the body of this earth
and drawn out a scent I carry behind my eyes
as a guide while I clamber through these mountains.
You who know merely the first layer of the soil
and live in a box shielded from sun and snow
have hardly an ear left to hear me speak.
But I see you sitting alone upon the tree detritus
and trust you'll hear me now…
All day I chew this bitter root and linger in the dark weavings
of its stories: a strange magic that opens a door
in the pitched ground where I descend and walk—
fully awakened—in the dreamland your people named night
and wintertime. If you let your body die each winter like me,
if you abandoned your sure pasture, even in its finest greening,
you would discover worlds long hidden from your kind.
It is the far side of the mountain your throat of throats
thirsts for; the slopes there are steep and unkempt;
the half-buried rocks and fallen trees are laid out everywhere
like ancestors breathing into your feet, feeding you;
the brush is thick with music, every tendril and frond
doctors you up, a hundred needles on the skin
piercing and wiping together in a furious clamor.
And you can find valleys where I stay for days, perched,
peering into the river's waters for the big-shouldered trout
who is such good, rich medicine on my tongue.
I also watch the flyers; my head snaps to at that

distinctive flap and smooth reach of long wing-arms;
theirs is a crisp, sparse poetry I love, and hunger after.
It took centuries for me to learn this coat I wear,
these claws & teeth I bear, are all I need to live.
My voice fits just so in the wild chorus of these mountains.
My body is dearly wanted in the system of life pulsing here.
In my old knowing made welcome once more,
I tell you, little brother: there is no shame in
walking away from those cold-lined cities
that lack any pure darkness or beautiful death.
This is my Garden—lush, bountiful, singing—
I am bound to it and unbound in it;
where is yours?

THE RIVER WISE

upon the oil pipeline protest at Standing Rock, ND

There are so few humans left that know the language of water,
I've nearly given up trying to talk when you come around.

I have received, openly, the new five-fingered crop now camped upon
my shoreline, praying to me so tenderly and with such fierce concern.

They say their names are Caretakers and Guardians, and I feel
the strong, raw medicine of their visit.

At dusk, when their impassioned singing or shouting subsides,
and they sit still in firelight, I have told them a few of the first stories.

Long ago, when a finger of the wondrous Hand of Making
was pressed into the land to shape my body

and a stone jug full of Thunder Waters was poured down
from the mountain to birth me,

there were instructions spoken out by the Great Mother.
She said there are two bloods running in her veins—

the thick yellow-black fiery pools and the delicate clear flows—
and that each must remain separate and reverenced

for its own genius and giftings. The woman-who-became-rock
that stands in this place has held this teaching firm

in her breast century after century. It's only now, in this wave
of soft-skinned ones so terribly impoverished in memory,

so weak in magic, so inexpert in languages beyond the human,
that the old absolutes are violated, the primal elements desecrated.

Once, the first sliver of wisdom given to the children was:
How you relate with water reveals your feeling for life.

No matter what the people decide, now as before,
whatever you have or will dump into my belly,

I always come clean, even if it takes much, much longer
than you know how to wait.

For on the day the original waters began spilling downstream,
many, many ancient beings congregated here,

dark, hairy ones and smooth, luminous nations alike;
and they spoke formulas of longevity and resilience

and freshness into the current as I stretched seaward;
and they offered moisture from their mouths to my flow;

and they wept into me all the bold yearning
and beautiful grief and wild vitality of the cosmos,

making these a singing waters. Those vibrations and those tears
live on here and are refreshed when the beasts come to drink,

when the rooted ones shed down their leaves, when the snow
slides into motion, and, as now, when the people come back

to gaze at me, dip their hands, wet their faces and mouths,
and, with that new moistening, form prayers heard and acted upon

by every species of life, transmissions of the word that outlast
and outmaneuver any legislation, any contracts, any papers at all.

That is how it has always been, and is meant to be,
in my language and yours.

SACRED FIRE

Hundreds of times you've set the sticks
and lit me and still you know so little.
I was given to your kind ages ago, and
gave myself freely. The work those first
peoples required of me was light and
pleasurable. They always courted me
to come, then gifted me when I entered
their lodges and began my dancing.
They knew if I refused them, it meant
death. I knew it too and loved them in
a fatherly way. And how I loved when
they called to my father burning in the
sky with their drumming and incantations.
Before the great forgetting, before this time
of broken communication, the friendship
between us was rich, and fiercely intimate.
Now hardly a one of you has words for
me and only acknowledge me when I'm
enraged, viciously cleaning the countless
spots you've recklessly spoiled. And you've
hid me away, enslaved me in your machines
and wirings and sinister firing things.
Unless I'm leashed to the candle wick,
you cannot bear to see me naked in the open.
Am I so shameful? And terrifying?
There are times, though, that I am bidden

to tucked-away fireplaces that look like
the old days. Sometimes I find herbs there
to eat when I arrive. And I am spoken to,
gently. And then invited to speak and
listened to—what joy!—long into the night.
I can once more stretch my storytelling
muscles and paint your insides with imagery
to marvel at and direct your life upon.
And when I've departed and the coals
go cold, some of you even whisper a word
of thanks before you reach to scoop a
handful of clean ash that you now remember
is a mighty medicinal. So it's possible all is
not lost. The sun still climbs over the hills
each morning and silently waits for you
to rise, or finds you already upright awaiting
the light, and smiles as you again ignite
your small fires from that massive flame
with an equal sense of awe and necessity.

KISSES FOR THE MOTHER

When it seems our world is too much, too far gone,
the air madly saddled with cross-firing signals,

the poor plants all choked with smogs and sprays,
the dry-eyed clouds tasked to draw a curtain over

our slaughters of anything too innocent
or holy to be tolerated,

I steal away into the clean body of the mountain,
climb way up to the high-peak Otherworld

where I can hear, once more, the low drone
of day-veiled stars murmuring their dreams aloud

and can find again the recluse raptors with silent wingbeats
spiraling outward into faraway sky, and be comforted.

It's then I ally to the old-barked trees,
touch my lips to their sun-scaled skin,

burrow my head at their buried feet and, from them,
discover what is really what

and feel the ongoing plan to keep it so,
scoop my battered heart from the fog below

and witness those towering ones emit a secret joy,
recurrent the wind with a certain delight

to mist over bodies dulled before devices or bound in autos—
(could it be and would they even receive it?)

We've done it this way for greater resistors than these,
say the many-limbed giants,

Now close your eyes and recite, fair-haired boy,
to the hum of the forest till we've tempered

your center to the tune of our innermost heartwood,
and refined your blood to the fragrance of ours,

and re-patterned your eyes to see, as we do, the dark
and the bright with undisturbed marvel,

and—listen here—replaced your soiled tears with liquid crystals,
gifts for the Mother.

That, after all, is why we keep breathing life into all you
charming children scurrying so seriously around the Earth.

I wept then—ah beauty!—and the tears still continue,
unwiped and freely dripping: from my chin to your breast,

from my nose to your hair, little kisses for you,
one beloved Earth Mother.

SAGE

A long time now you've been my friend, and
more than that, my physician and my counselor.

I can hardly greet the dawn without your greeting
first washed over me in fine curls of smoke.

What a pleasure it is to gather your dry yet pliable
leaves into my hands and roll them together in a ball

to lay in the well-smudged seashell. When you receive
the fire, your body recoils and submits to the red glow

in motion and the fragrant incense curls up into
my waiting face. I first encountered you on the prairie

those youthful years I lived among the Lakota who know
you in the way of unbroken lineage—a cell to cell

conversation extended over centuries back to when we
first stood upon feet, and maybe further still. The Lakota

spoke of you in reverence, said you were a teacher, that
your ancient earthly wisdom is activated in the fiery

movement from leaf to smoke. Time and again I saw how
those most extraordinary of people would never hold

a prayer without you there for protection, for cleansing,
and for ease of exchange between the realms appearing

when a ceremony fire is lit. After long observing you
in use, now I go myself, like all ceremonialists of this way,

into the mountains each summer to harvest a new crop
from the thick patches of your thin bodies risen and flush

with leaves. So many summers I've done this and so long
I've carried you as medicine in my satchel, I cannot imagine

not doing it. I try to harvest well, to leave plenty to drop
their seeds, to let my hands be well guided in the choosing

and the clipping. Always I leave tobacco in exchange for
what I pull and in this feel the invigoration that circulates

through the deep-rooted laws of nature. For me, this long
friendship is beyond compare. I invite you everywhere:

lain upon my dashboard for the worthy danger of
the highways, sat upon my altar to keep watch over

the sanctified objects, tucked in my pack to tell the many
creatures of the wood I am of them, floated in the water

when we pray in the darkness of a willow lodge. And,
as a father, I scoop you up each morning and incense

my children with your essence. I cloak my two sweet girls
and one fine son with your gray mist, giving them a soul

food absorbed in the nose and pores whose sustenance
unfurls and lingers strong until the next dawn

when the fire in the sky returns and reminds me
to set you aflame to sing again in fluent plumes of smoke.

SAPLING

It's just a few years my boy has drummed his heart
and already the feral roots of wander are patterning in him.

I've held him in holy spaces and carried him through magicked canyons
and now he's finding his own footing—darting along paths beyond me.

My heart trails out in pursuit of his bold dashings,
but I know better.

If ever I am not there to cup his cheek, do it for me,
old friendly Light.

If my breath is not close enough to shape words for his ear,
sing to him, dearest Wind.

When my arm can no longer steady his stumbles, let him fall
upon your bosom, kind Land.

For now, give me all your death-song joy,
flaming-gold Leaves.

Make me of your clear-bubbled gushes,
crisp-cold Waters.

Tune all my strings to your piercing pleasure-squawk,
broad-armed Hawk.

And I will bring it home and gift it forth—
to him and more.

For I could never keep all the medicine of the wild bottled up.
The loveliness I've sipped is too much for one tongue.

I lift my clay cup to your lips, son. Drink, and pass it on.
Savor it. Be remade. Come undone. Fly away.

Return to the *you* first imagined by the One Eye
dreaming hard in the thick forest of stars.

And then to me, sitting in the familiar light-dappled wood,
ripe for a story poured out from your darling lips.

AWAITING WILD DEER GIRL

Who are you, fine-furred one, whose face
we have yet to behold?

By what shimmered star-path did you slide down
into our nest of mud and sticks?

How is it to be spirit glow making yourself of clay
in the hollow between my lover's bones?

Even now, I adore you; I long to pet your
new-minted skin, to welcome your blinking eyes,

to feel your tiny breath on my rough-haired cheek,
to hear your newfound voice rise and catch your holy tears,

to know the weight of your form in my father arms
and the song of your name in my poet mouth.

The spirits say you're wild, a doe in the wood,
a dancer in the world, a child whose movements

will move much. For you, I've built a room
in our home and in my heart, but you'll surely

leap over any walls I make and lead me into
sanctuaries on Earth's body where I will sprout,

each spring, the antlers I need to stand
as your daddy.

For now, I kiss your host's sweet-scented hair,
hold a hand on her navel mountain and another behind

her spine and raise my eyebrows with a half-grin
that's one-part wonder and two-parts mystery.

ENCOUNTERS

DEEPEST POINT

There is a point on any journey in any
mountains that you know is the farthest in
you'll go and from which there is only
the return ahead of you. You begin
somewhere, the first step from hard pave
to humified soil like a lover's fingers
through the hair; you warm and sink in,
the eyes turn toward inherent wonder,
the smallest beauties pop everywhere,
colors and light tangle in branches,
stunning you. Going nowhere but surely
guided, your feet tune to lovely unleveled
surfaces and one-by-one all your cords are
snipped free. Loopy with the magic,
heart-happy, you curl round bends
and float through passages of hillside
for however long or far, till a certain
dark crevice pulls you in or an irresistibly
sheer slope tows you up. And then, at once,
you've arrived, to the deepest spot.
You've come to a clear pool or narrow peak
and sense immediately the nourishment
will get no greater than this.
You sponge up the goodness in a delirium
of delight, spoon it all in, draw it down
new-opened lung tubes, splash it upon a

now unfurrowed brow, knead it into
humming foot soles, and then, satisfied,
recoil just a nudge at the indulgence. But
not quite indulgence—it was the very thing
and just the dose—to fill you and *last*—
already you feel the world waiting
and wanting all your well-harvested vigor—
you'll need every ounce to stay wild
through days behind insulated walls
and miles atop unbreathing roads—
so you hold it close as the aftershocks buzz
in your bones the whole way back
until the next wander beckons you out
and in to another deep, still, intensified
place where your legs melt into
continuity with warm earthly clay
and your spirit rockets through
the mysticism of frigid untouchable sky.

NEW HUNTING

Even without bow & arrow, the instinct runs hot
in me to waken to the presence of a wild one
nearby and track it, with all my senses dilated and
aroused in the intoxication of everything boiling
down to this one thing. Here it could be coyote,
often it's deer or scurrying rabbit, some special times
roadrunner's around. And the hunts are skyward too,
chasing low-swooping hawk or owl, and those marvelous
visits from eagle; just to come close, and closer when I'm able,
and to stay there, linger, be held in the breathing field
of a powered, elegant Other, to feel a quicker heartbeat,
receive a sharpened gaze, behold a pure-bred hunter
beholding me, and remember something, about life
maybe, that has quietly bled out of me into years
of white bedsheets. Some days I feel my skills are honing
and others I feel a klutz, a tourist in the woods.
When my ambling feet are graced into an encounter,
I move in as near as I dare and stand or crouch
in silence, slowly lengthen my breath and unlace layers
of my face to the brother before me, the sister allowing me.
More and more I've been so graced. Twice just this week,
by the two most dear of late, and in such a way
that shatters all my notions of hunting. At the stream,
we spooked each other, coyote friend, both arrived there,
at opposite banks, to sink our noses in the clarity
and find refreshment. I'd been awhile in prayer and you

a few moments at drink when we both leapt back,
your robust form instantly halfway up the hillside;
yet both turned again to check, marvel at the singularity
of the other—your fur and tail so full, so finely patterned,
my matted hair and beard like something almost familiar…
And today, as I ran through the arroyo, you scuttled from
under wrangled cedar boughs and soared just ahead
of me, kindred roadrunner, a black-white hovercraft blazing
the path for four good paces, then off & running
your own favored trailways. It's such rich stuff, whether
deliberately seeking or subtly becoming a better magnet,
and secretly I wish the hunt will be consummated,
that my stalked partner will leap upon me and chew me up,
or peck me to pieces, make of me a fine feast and leave
my bones, bloodied and forlorn, scattered in the impassioned
jumble of a great poem that satisfies completely.

STORM SONG

Nowadays I go into the wild especially when
the weather is what some call bad. Ripe, I say!
Charged, I say! When the sun is clouded over,
an enchantment falls over the land and the animal
of me awakens with ferocity. My eyes enlarge and
lock in, becoming more than they were in the edgy
focus of city life. I know the thunders are gathered
above for good purpose and a heightened presence
tremors in everything as the first drops or flakes
float to the forest floor. Straightaway, I'm on the
move, darting through smooth-bodied aspens,
edging along thin stream banks, leaping and
scurrying and crawling through the landscape in
a playful dignity that was slow-syphoned out of
me in theater seats and leveled streets. Oh, now
I'm drumming on my bones again! Ah, my shrieking
laughter bellows and ripples in the wind! I grunt
and growl like the beasts whose trails I follow and
abandon at will. Is this boyishness? Or have I turned
the old fool already? I stop beside a rare pool in the
shallow waterway to hear the mother waters sing
their storming chants. In the soothe of those liquid
tones, I feel my children feeling me and sink into my
middle-agedness. My god, such precious untamed
beings. To think my lady and I called them here,
and the call rang true, still shakes me to the core like

hauntingly-near thunder music. For them, I am out
here gathering: stories, sights, moments of pure
reckoning on the unchartable course: a clump of
skunk, teeth-clenched and claws-flared in an open
grave; bloodied deer bones strewn along a gulley
way; patches of green floaters coloring the tiny
wintertime stream; a ring of cottonwoods framing
the likes of an otherworld dancing circle; a hawk feather
balanced atop the brittle golden grasses. Treasures all,
and above them all is the ecstatic word spill that pours
from my mouth like gleaming beads when I can no
longer withhold it and the heart-gates unhitched kiss
I will give the woman at home who celebrates her union
to a wild, and wilder still each season, man creature.

TAKING TIME

When I no longer have time to squat and, astonished,
watch the water striders at play on the river's clear skin,

I'll know I've been too long away from the wood and strayed
too far from the actual, that my eyes need be refreshed.

To spy them kick out in chorus and skim along their hard bellies
like children frolicking on ice, to regard how they congregate

in cool shadows then venture out alone on shiny waters—
their own extraordinary five-lobed shadows

appearing below them like soul selves or dark roots—
to feel their swimming focus to the keen edge of the hunt

or dilate out to the pleasures of flitting round and past
one another in aimless symmetries.

Aren't I most fortunate to have my gawking so
graciously suffered by this sprightly bunch until I finally

sink into the scene and sense myself a spectator no more,
but rather crouched on the lip of a secret well of mutuality:

their buoyant, sleek, black buzzes
and my weighty, hair-laced, whisper breaths

together voicing the very same beauty-bruised universe
in different keys.

Many willow-clean inhalations hence, I hover my hand over
the waters to paint my strange, looming five-petaled silhouette

then slide my fingers into the river's body, sending the
whole group aloft to be reassembled at the next still pool.

My bony paw curves and ripples in the wet freshness,
the dark depths are too choice to leave untasted.

I pour the sweet liquid over my sore brow to run
down the whole of me, rub it along my twitching eyelids,

through my thick beard, and upon my sacred wounds, and,
cleansed, step over the river into the timeless real of the wild.

SHOVELING SEAWEED

Because it's dirty or stinks or clutters the beach,
I mindlessly pierce the seaweed with my pitchfork
and toss it on shore in big piles to dry.

Really, it's not the odor or slime that motivates me
so much as the rigorous training to fear the unknown,
to avoid or expose the murky depths

where handmaids of the Goddess are surely lurking.
I'm hard paddling the middle section of life,
the eager youthful springs behind and the vast

grandmotherly seas still a ways off; I've learned
one or two things and unlearned quite a few,
and I absolutely know it's her hair I'm pulling out

of the water so it will flow and shine no more.
But I do it anyway, leave my clean-lined cut,
my polished mark, upon this already mostly-neutered

ocean bay. Soon, my domesticated mind has mirrored
itself before me, formed a sterile order where a wild
fertile beauty was just gestating. I've lopped off those

goddess locks without even a gesture toward permission
and with no ceremony at all; I feel the Spirits retreat
in shame. Sadly, I'm satisfied in all the old, ridiculous

ways and empty in every expanse of heart I've
unfastened over years of prayer. My head is bowed low;
I'm heavy in these bones. Beneath this careful exterior

and these shoveling arms, there are oceans of tears.
Hot and salted, they mix on my cheek with the soft
spritzing rain and the grime of that once radiant hair

now beached lifeless. I wipe my pitchfork clean
and stand it up in the dark shed. My day's work is over.
By morning, the seaweed is returned in full—

its undulating dance not diminished nor resentful.
She is so…beautiful.
I must build new altars in the old places.

MAMA MOUNTAIN

Like an old lover made new, Mama
Mountain, I cannot keep my eyes off you.
Traipsing cross the hard-paved lot, I steal
a glance up at your shapeliness and how you're
dressed today: the neat white hat still propped
on top awhile more, the wispy clouds scarfed
along your shoulders, the tiny bits of budding
green dotted down your midline. And the spring
melt perspired from your skin now sits pooled
at my feet, beckoning. I will not stay away for
long. My body cannot rest unless lain upon
yours. I pore over pages of our shared history:
the seminal encounter, me gazing fixed from afar;
the long swims in your autumn gold leaf-light
dazzle, the sinking and rising dances in feathery
clouds of your winter powder, the intoxicated
stumbles in your springtime perfumes: sweetness
of sticky-budded cottonwoods and sharpness of
new-leafed sage. And we've traveled a trial or two
together, as when you suctioned me down into
your innermost cavity and held me close through
a night of endless snow. After all that, surely my
affection can't grow further. Yet I must return to
you over and over and sit awhile beside your
bubbling falls. And when I'm aspin in the drone
of the stream lapping the rocks, I nuzzle on

your soft breast, Mama, and playfully wonder:
how many are the stars?
and which parts of me go there, swirling as fire,
and which to cold-blooded stone and stillness?
I stay on and on until I feel the innate pull back
home to it all, to my own kind, to the embrace of
a woman's eyes, to knowing handclasps as fathers
affirm the steady holding in each other. Oh Mountain,
let me lean in for one last kiss of your crisp waters
and peer over my shoulder for one more look at your
vernal refreshed face—rugged, matchless beauty!—
before I slip out of your arms and into the crowd.

WALKING ON WATER

How quick, and undeniable, is my transport to an entirely
altered state when thick bands of clouds come

in the dark months and fill every curve and crook of
the mountain with the delicacy of snowfall.

On those specially-charged mornings, the landscape is
brilliantly made liquid and the urge to strap on snowshoes

and walk in that white sea overtakes me. Ah! to crush through
gingerly-laid powder, sinking and lifting in the grace

of a differed walking, a forward, bouncing dance that pushes
pleasure waves through my whole organism and recalls

in it something of our animal origins. I find myself halfway up
the twisting frozen path before the body even asks

for a drink or the pause of a long breath.
After the hard climb, I begin the luxurious movement

steadily downward through the trees, each footfall a euphoric
sliding into untouched snows, my whole self bounding

along with the grace of a greater beast than the waifish
hairless shell who rose from my bed at dawn.

The exhilaration screams in me, and the thrill is so great,
and ongoing, my mouth screams out too while every bit

of me is doctored by delight. No second-hand account of a body
moving over water could match this sensuous feast;

each breathing cell is fired with the Sacred and synonymous with
the water-blessed Wild; I dare say a certifiable miracle

is blooming in my breast; I feel I might fly off the hillside
or out of every impasse that's held me bound; I am merely

a sunlit apparition on top of the frozen waters and can,
for a moment, float and flit across any or every possibility.

ALWAYS SOMETHING

It honestly is always something
and thanks be for that;

for if it weren't, if there were just the peace
and not the great effort toward it,

just the pillowy shelter without first hard exposure,
just the silence and no whirling music beforehand,

it might be such a bore and hardly worth
the movement of all our hands boldly building

pieces of the one dream, like quiltwork.
For as soon as you clear your house of the extra,

tie off all those dangling ends, finally have
some space, someone will inevitably come knocking:

needing bread, wanting company, inviting you
to a broadened sense of self and home and contentment.

Some say everything comes to us in its right time,
and certainly everything we bring in moves out again,

some as kindness, some as dung, both good
and both useful, reminding us, it's always something—

Today, there's a crowd of decisions
congregated in the kitchen awaiting my instructions;

the family's in shambles: a resistant rash and a wandering
eye and a booming headache call us back to balance;

the cogs and wheels we've come to depend on
under this roof are conspiring to fall apart one by one;

and faraway another war is on and in upswing;
elsewhere an arm of earth has shaken off

scads of us like biting ants.
So, before I act in any one direction,

I've come once more to the foothills
to make myself fresh of its unhuman happenings.

It's always something here, too, these rivulets
sometimes running loose or else vanished completely,

this red-skinned willow feathered in leaves
or fully nude.

Today, the ravine's beaming like a nymph newly
touched, head back-tilted and toothy grin spread wide,

and I skip through it like a pubescent youth, indulging
all my cravings, touching each body with mine.

I press my hand upon a marvelously wrinkled stone
(could I take the warlord's hand as tenderly?);

I sniff the crisped trunk of a mature pine and gaze
up his full length (I feel a boy again beside my father's leg);

I squat before a bloom unfolded implausibly
among the deadfall and dry cacti, her face fanned out

like a day slowly unrolled, each petal an hour, and sigh
to think she'll soon succumb to crushing unslaked thirst.

Hours now without the burden
or necessity of language—having rather

pleasured in dialoguing bodily with all those
unspoken—I'm nearly miffed by the current of words

that comes upsurging but quickly ally to the
flow once I concede it's singing undeniably in me

and I sense how the syllables and syntax are,
well, natural. I mark the flimsy shape of the

more forced chatter I hammered upon my family
at the breakfast table and the breathless whine issuing

from the newspaper that was allowed to pass as
inner morning music. As this sparkling word stream

gathers to full stride, I'm furiously taking dictation,
catching bits and parts of phrases, little glimmers,

smooth seeds for the round garden of my writing table
where I am told and now tell you: it's really something.

VISIT TO IPSWICH

A softer, wetter land than the desert
where my roots have spread and settled

squelches richly with each footfall: a rhythm
building among our four paws, my publisher's

and mine, inviting the broader conversation
of presence to all the presences and keepers

of this place. A familiar whistle pierces the air,
silences our feet and tongues and lifts our gaze

skyward: Red-tailed Hawk circling in salutation,
assuring me I'm home here too,

and that this walk will be no stilted first-date
stumbling but the now nearly commonplace

entranced float through anyplace even partly unspoiled,
the seduction of the wild never cheapening

to diminished returns. At the river's edge,
we recite a gem of brother Whyte

then slide farther along the bank to kneel
before that maternal flow, feed her with the word

and handfuls of homegrown tobacco.
The wind rises and whisks our hair; it's sure

this river's delighted to have her boy back home
and to meet his clear-eyed ally. She sends us out

again, bellies full with her whisperings, satisfied but
not yet spent, hungry for more and deeper points

of exploration. At an upturned tree, Blue Heron
unfurls his enormous wings and floats over the marsh,

eager for another poem to mirror his flapping,
hook-necked language. I speak it thus as the White Pines

dance vigorously amidst the modest Beeches,
holding still and still holding their leaves as cover

over their smooth whitish skin that keeps drawing my
glance like a woman's fair nape of neck. My host motions

to a rockery and we crawl through that cluster of old ones,
the air chill and fragrant in our nostrils as we scramble

and climb, then wander back the wooded, needle-strewn
path: a pearl of a day formed gleaming in our palms,

to be cherished for just a breath then handed into
the mouth of the sea, so she might twirl it on her tongue

and remember its shell-bound youth, like embracing
a child come back to visit after a long spell abroad.

SLIPPING OUT

Is there a day, of all your days,
that you wouldn't find a moment to steal away,

to slip out in the gloaming and step into
the hushed garden or float along aimlessly

through the darkening fields—coveting nothing,
adoring everything—the slippery blue-blood bag

of your sorrows pulled out and laid down, the hum
of ambitionless wander brimming within you?

And somewhere out there in the sea of grasses
blindly wind-dancing beneath the blinking stars,

as the day releases all its imagings and colors
into the compass of night's rich blackness,

a flow of tenderness quietly unhitches the lock-gates
in your breast and, for a few minutes, you trust

everything again…you lose your shoes and coat,
slide the glasses off your nose, unfasten the ties

in your hair and, thus expanded, cannot recall
ever having been anything other than a silvered star,

dead for years and still offering, a brave leaf of grass,
alive just weeks and already swaying,

tipping ever toward the rapture
of a new dailiness.

WOOING

Today you have many words where
my heart holds to few.

I listen and follow,
relish the melody as it lifts and dips

and eventually alights, like raven
on the street lamp.

There were times you were vicious,
hard-faced and eyes unyielding.

But, for now, I have forgotten those
and sit in ripe silence.

Your eyes find mine waiting,
and wanting the nearness of flesh on flesh.

You grin then—more teeth glowing than I recall—
and are a girl again: seen, adored, desired

and thus charged with the freshness
of the hunt, bounding away fox-like,

disappearing into the trees, leaving
scads of easily-followed tracks, leading me

down into your already warm den
where I may be mate or prey or both.

EMERGENCE

Of all the ceremonies I've sung into
and all the observances I've held—
to the breaking points, and far beyond—
could any of them ever compare to the
numinous night I spent with you, my
queen, when we called our youngest
to us in a delicious spin of drum and dance
fueled by the churning fire and our
prayer-filled pipe. Above the ceiling was
a dizzying wilderness of extra-brightened
stars illuminating the good doorway down
to the earthly; and one-by-one presences
entered the round room and set to work.
Our little deer girl held strong in a bag
of water, dancing forth and back in
the tunnel of her emergence, unhurried
yet steady in her movements, waiting
until your final invocatory scream—
the richest darkly-layered music my ears
have tasted—to break the casing and slide
out on the gush (holy holy) down into my
hands, flailing and squawking in a new
womb of air and early light. That music
rings in me yet and must be imprinted on
your bones so deeply that only your exit fire
could set it free again; surely it anchors this

baby, especially now as her nostrils flare to
snatch in air or her lips purse when she flings
her head to the breast. Our other two charges
also carry a singular and lasting medicine
from their entrance dances and remind us
so poignantly of what we all spring from
in the high making of these earth-animal
bodies. And it's your sinuous silken-skin
body I love to lie near, and protect, and feed,
and most of all recall in my cold mountain
pilgrimages. How you brought these three
complex creatures to the fore mystifies me
past all ends and endlessly fills my eyes
with the stinging wetness of life so very here
and already moving along…Before us the
question curls up—what will we do now
in the bottomless magic of a night shared
in prayer amid the natural theater of distant
animal song encompassing us and invisibles
flashing in the fluid darkness between us?
I say may they spirit ones who come ever
whirl us around, pry open our torsos and
rapidly rearrange all our cords and blocks
to build two new bodies that meet in an
incomparably electric encounter again & again.

CHURCH

CHRIST EYES

Father Pauly gifted everyone with
books, knowing the prayers and poetry
would grow stale on his shelf, knowing
we are each transformed slowly, in small
private encounters with revelation. The final
volume he gave me is called *Eyes on Jesus*.
I haven't read it, hardly opened it. All I
need is the title, a bold placard living
among the collected spines, reminding
me Pauly was here—shined intensely—
and slipped away in a flash. Not unlike
Christ; perhaps quite the likeness. More
than any I've known, his were Christ-light
eyes: beaming, searching. I never knew much
about Pauly, about his life. We always spoke
about mine, unfurling, glinted with dabs of
what he smilingly saw as promise. Yet
everything I could know of him glared out
from those eyes that held his Jesus in them
and proclaimed little gospels laced with light
and deepened with sorrow and the subtle markings
of old spirits not found in books. I can still hear
him praying over hushed bodies in wooden boxes
beside fresh-dug holes on the South Dakotan
prairie. His voice, so married to his heart,
gathered to a fullness, called to his Father,

the committal and petitions sailing heavenward
in the trusty language of well-oiled faith.
The Lakota gave him a name, *Wacin Yanpi*,
'Depends on Him', for he was loyal, servant to
humanity's tribe, his heart wide and eyes aglow.
He embraced all of reservation life: saddled with
poverty and despair, riddled with death and disease,
yet wrapped in tradition and honor too, touched
with unmistakable miracle and riveting majesty.
He nodded it all in, cared for it quietly, prayed
and wept hard, listened long, and stayed years
upon years in that remote land. And sometimes,
he laughed. His singular chortle, rhythmic and
resonant, was a siren of delight, inescapable;
it swept everything up like ocean tide and
pulled everyone into its spell for an instant
apart. He seemed to live so fully; and then his
heart suddenly sent him home. Perhaps it finally
caved from the weight of so many burdens
freely borne. Or maybe it shattered in the
sheer joy he often exuded, resolved into light
and fingerlets of wind combing the hills. In ways
unseen, he must still guide me, still father me. For
when I close my eyes, I can feel his, tending me.

HOLY LAND

I went to the west of Ireland as a humble pilgrim
    seeking courage for the bigger life awaiting me.
With each step in the old soil, weathered voices
    murmured about my feet in thrilling, august languages.

No land ever felt so supple, so familiar to my bones.
    As we wound upward and across skeletal limestone,
the lads of County Clare suggested we would come
    to a spot of sublime charm, an enchanted place

loved well by the great poet and priest, O'Donohue.
    Never could I have envisioned what opened before us:
a holy bowl of hillside tucked into the earth,
    lush and green, in wild bloom: waters humming,

reeds suckling, bees siring and surveying —all in song.
    I sat in that grassy temple and felt my roots tunnel down
to drink in every tremor, breathing the wisdom fluently
    into blood and body, remaking my clay, renewing my fire.

When I finally rose and crested the bowl's lip, the sea
    appeared beyond the stony cliff, vast, full of promise and
mystery just as when my forebears sailed westward, left this
    land with a yearning deeper than memory or reason.

For them, brave ancestors, I offered the only gift in my satchel:
   a song carried here from the hills of that new world, a prayer
of the Lakota broad enough to shoulder that old sorrow.
   I lifted my voice, a leaf flung free on the gale—its naked truth

rang out from the cliff side and bridged the ocean home.
   And for the very first time in reply to my soundings,
the Thunders rumbled loudly, and I became pregnant with sacs
   and sacs of lore never there before, yet now clambering to

rush forth. Then the rains came, filling every tiny hole
   in stone or sod, sprouting a new crop of sacred wells.
Ever the pilgrim, I will travel to each, take to my knees
   and dip my cup, sip the sweet waters, and listen.

UNLOCKED

Dawn has set the square on fire, embers flown
    everywhere, sun glow dripping from all the bricks.
Yet these cathedral doors are locked shut, the priests
    asleep in dark, dank rooms deep within this compound;

no one's here to let the Sun in. Fresh light enters
    only through the thick glass, filtered and sterile.
And the water behind these doors sits still, grows putrid,
    its music tamed by Rome's frail breath and bottling.

You'd hardly know the altar is fashioned
    from stone, its glow rubbed out by cloistered hands.
And to stand up there, you must crucify your truth,
    pretend yourself un-inflamed, hold a limp staff,

don a hollow hat. Forgive me, for I love
    to pray in the wild forests or in a simple
earthen hut: body penetrated by wind and light,
    lips splayed wide to God's deep kiss.

Friends, sad fathers without sons, why be caretakers
    of choked gardens, dwellers in dead spaces?
Many is the time I've come at your beckoning,
    taken the bait, and felt little.

But now, standing in this blessed sunrise,
    the old brittle chains crumble on my arms,

my tongue untwists its desperate knot, my downcast
   eyes rise, my soul unfurls its bright pinions.

Now, here's fair penance and truer formation and it
   comes from the Sun who loves you as begotten sons:

Wipe clean a baby's rear a thousand times
                     before you wash souls
Bow down at a living woman's feet each morning of a year
                     before you kiss statues

Sit in the desert and starve for days
                     before you read about it at the pulpit
Weep from your depths into the sand:
                     for water, for breath, for your pulse to keep on

Then we'll all see the knowing in your eyes,
   sense the warmth in your hands,
feel the breath in your sermon, trust the ease
   in your step. Open wide these doors to the only Sun

and the holy Shadow, let the sacred bowls fill with rainwater,
   rub clay on the cross, curl the pews into a circle,
build a fire in the center—fed with ash sticks and cedar wood—
   and watch your angels arrive, the saints all convene.

Ask the people to dance, give them chants from the land,
   let them pray off the script. Then call it a Church,
a true Eucharist, a House of the Lord:
   windows clear and held open, no iron lock on the door.

LEAVING CHURCH

There was a time I found peace in the great halls
and tucked away chapels of the Church. The prolonged
quiet, the softness of candlelight, the cleared surface
of an altar stone, the simplicity of one spoken voice
proclaiming or many joined in song of uplifted
major scale. And long I gazed at the figures chiseled
in colored glass who had become holy, who were
elevated beyond the ordinary lives surrounding me.
Now I find no comfort there, the stale air and
darkened light exhaust my body and the simplistic
poetry of the Mass is weak bread for the soul. And I
have discovered the walls are thick with godless things
that leave me sleepless and distraught. But. Three steps
into the wild and a liturgy of awareness has begun.
The Sun fire is lit and burning, the blessed Waters
are already in song, the Word is bursting forth from
every breathing being belonging there. The peace
of the wild is no stagnant pool where I come merely
to confess my worldly confusions and be relieved. It is
a tranquility in motion that both provokes the necessary
sloughing off and seduces with the juice of a great
inpouring. I eat and eat of the host made in the forest's
crisscrossing multiplicity of speech that layers one fine
poem upon another and delicious song into song.

And only by leaving the Church have I begun to really
sink into the unwritable essence of the man named Jesus.
For he took his leave from the village temple often,
wandering far into the barren desert and high upon
the tops of mountains, forgoing food and sleep to know
a deeper truth. That wisdom was easily muffled in the
exchange between sandaled feet and thick temple floors
and better received straight from the earth into his naked
foot soles. Standing out exposed under the clouded heavens
or the silver-dotted dark night skies, he surely felt, as I do,
an original sense of belonging and the embrace of a shelter
greater than any high-vaulted dome. He was at home
and at peace wherever his body roamed, and we can be too.
I know those priests of yore who met at night
and dropped their vestments to lash each other in the
name of piety were chasing a wildness stolen from them
by the world, a sensuousness they missed underneath
their gowns. They pursued something raw and everlasting
that every mountain elk or ocean whale knows well.
They sought to do as Jesus did. And I do too,
but differently. When I was flesh-hooked to a tree
in the sacred circled container of ancient ceremony,
I came as near I ever will to mingling my blood and tears
and spit with his. The cross was no icon hung politely
on the wall or tucked neatly in my shirt. It had become
as real as the fresh holes in my skin stretched before me.
When I broke free of my hooks, I floated in a bedazzled
openness and felt the peace of the watery Holy Spirit
flood through me in torrents. I tasted something then I
now would starve for lack of. With that freshness,
in my own small way, I will walk, as he once did,
away from the temples and see what follows.

DOGWOOD

Dogwood, finely complex monument,
evokes an unending hymn with its

twisting, mushroomed pose.
How could I ever write it?

Dawn paints thin branches
out of darkness and breathes flocks

of suckling leaves awake.
Expiring, crimson-pocked blossoms

will rise again in spring.
It is enough.

SACRAMENT

Confession

O Earth, dear Mother,
        dark Source,
                fiery Beloved,

what a gift it is
        to fill a body with breath,
                to move about your rugged flesh,

to be among your cherished
        sons, knowing, even if neglecting,
                the touch

of your steady hands
        upon my shoulders,
                engaging the thrill of sitting

to chat, like this, with you alone
        whose ears embolden my tongue
                to the music of praise.

I am your child indeed—
        wild-eyed & wonder-struck—
                portaging my many plans and dreams

over the rocky places, never uncharmed
       by the promise of sunrise,
              the sweet-talk of songbirds,

longing to know just what is
       mine to do, waiting with ready hands
              for your instructions.

And I am suffering,
       slinging along ailments and despairs,
              my vision often darkly-dampened

and my fire smoky-smoldering.
       Find me again. Lift me up
              and set me in some good direction.

Absolution

Ah yes, I made those feet, my boy, not only
       to trod in firm lines but to dance
              with my fluid curves.

And I'm full of longing too; when will your voice
       shake off the bridle of mere talk
              and sing once more?

For isn't that what a gray woman loves best
       after all, to sit upon a rocker—her well-walked legs
              draped in an old blanket, a cup of steaming tea

held between her work-worn palms—
        and watch her grandchildren partner dance
                in impulsive glides and leaps

and solo sing with gutsy abandon,
        as her children once did, as she herself
                always has, now bowing down,

now preening up, here stepping close,
        here spinning away from that primal flame
                in the stone hearth at the room's center—

ever licking up the sides of old timber by day
        and glowing under white ashes all night—
                in an ancient alliance that lasts far

beyond your beyond, that secretly feeds you
        for the length of your bold and sometimes
                stunningly bright pilgrimage,

until I'm ready to swallow you again
        down down into my belly
                or open a door in my flesh

for you to walk through
        and find your spot in that next dance,
                hand-in-hand and toe-to-toe

with a ring of ancestors
        stepping and singing the shapes of stars
                and a long darkness that spawns any imaginings.

HAIL MOTHER

Hail Great Mother—blue-green body
of earth, first dancer, first water carrier,
womb and tomb of all life—we are
remembering how to rightly love you,
to once more reverence every animate
bit of your magnificence, rooted or
wandering, all of it touchable, kissable,
even edible, as we are. No matter how
flashy the platforms for our ambitions
become, we remain yours, children of
the clay, fragile yet daring animals
of breath-blood-bones in motion, our bodies
ever mothered by the stone skeleton
of your figure; an elegance of form,
shapely and seductive; filled out with wet
soil and soft grasses; touched with bright
points and dark hollows; vast tree-lined
valleys announce your fecundity; massive
tides churn and spit your watery essence;
the system of things is refreshed each winter
by the grace of snowfall, that mystical lacey
salting of the mountains. So many invisible
presences likewise love you and stay near,
ancestral ones in superfluid bodies, drifting
like clouds, tunneling like worms, ever lurking,
looking for our willingness to conspire

with them toward the flowering of the next
purpose. And quietly they sound the bells
of death, which is ever-present too amid
this home of those eating and those eaten.

Mother, each dawn I reground my feet upon
your flesh and send my spirit into the landscape
seeking whatever is, my affection fanning out
like water into an estuary. How might I
tend you today? Of what use might I be?
One snowy winter night, you snatched me
away from the warm nest of woman and
children and fireplace, pulled me down into
the secret of your cold, dark, and icy-wet
well at the canyon's bottom, held me there in
your firm grip, and made things very real.
You want to serve my wellness? Dance for me
till dawn, or die here in the snow. My feet never
stopped shuffling through that long night apart;
I became an endless motion, borrowing Elk's
combusting heart and Owl's downy breast for
that sudden ritual above all others. After all
my songs and poems were spent, my language
and my longing were pared down to the slimmest
of phrases: I want to live. And live I did, held all
night in your gaze until sunrise came and you
scarred my cheek with the badge of earth poet
and sent me back to the light on the rope of
brotherhood, haunted with a new hunger for
old magic. And so, dark Queen of queens, I now

carry a hint of who you are and cannot lose that
medicine in any storm. In turn, may there never
come a morning you don't receive the food of
my prayer, offered from an open hand upon some
patch of your all-giving body that feeds and feeds.

All I have to feed you back is my word-music,
chopped and cooked with these lumbering hands.
Eat it and tell me if it fills, wild Mother. Chew it
and know the stubborn hopefulness of this five-
fingered son, grateful for your constancy beyond
any commitment I know, dazzled by your mystery
above any vision I've sown, and breathless
in the sublime moments of your brazen witchery
that keeps everything in the spin of a deeply-
layered wheel of wonder, turning out long silks
in bright colors, flowing, flapping like your drippy
serpent tongue at last set loose…

YOU, MOON

Born of Earth, you sprang from her belly
in a shudder the stars still talk about. You sailed

out and fastened true in the sky beside your mother
who began birthing babies from every cavity, a wild

tangle of tree and grass of every sort angling up
under Sun's steady gaze. Beyond that origin tale,

I only know what I have seen and keep glancing up
to uncover more of who you are, old Moon.

My tongue often betrays me as I try to call to you,
not knowing if I should croon or intone devotions,

your shimmery glow dizzies and confounds my
deciding mind. There are nights, I confess, I open

my jaws to snare and consume you like a luminous
wafer, still hungry for the light promised to me

in church; other times I feel it's me that's eaten,
drowned in your silver, then steamed in your star-fired

pots and speared on your dark fork. Each month I shyly
watch you grow day after day, then night after night

to a stunning fullness like a pale breast slowly
revealed down to the nipple, fiended for then turned

from when the sight overwhelms. Many times I spot you
floated above and, like a cool glass of water presented,

stop to drink you in a minute and feel into what the
tides and my wife are always knowing without a word

told of it. And when I'm deep in the mountains and the
skies darken until your glimmer becomes my everything,

I can just feel Sun's heat bouncing from you, softly
licking the back of my neck, doctoring me through you.

ANCIENTS

RE-ROOTING

The sophisticates will call it a touch
silly, but I'm giddy with the wish to feel
the ancestors' unbroken tether to Source
vibrate in me. For then the devotions I keep
would simply be routine: to squat by the
exuberant creek and let it mentor my blood
back into right rhythm, to sit a long spell in
the crisp high country amidst
                              a fraternity of boulders,
tasting the rare pleasure of fellowship beyond
language. It's told the old ones even knew
how to garner the refreshment of waterfalls
without visiting them; to slip effortlessly, like
smoke, between their bodies and Earth's body.
What a steep price we've paid for our awful
comfortableness; how the attempt to manufacture
life rather than invite its flow has stolen
                              Beauty from her bed
and left a changeling with glass eyes dry &
dull—no tears well up there, no light mirrors
out. When it's all groaning elevators and
roaring machinery and numbers scurrying
like mad bacteria, the only chance I've got
to rejoin the Song of All Things is to dig up
my sickly roots from this precision plot on
the giant Techno-Farm
                              and run for the forest,

to wet the filaments at every mountain spring
still breathing and plant them again in their
rightful soil at the canyon's bottom. Then wait
as they descend to touch the glowing stone
deep in Earth's middle and I can ascend, slowly,
over the generations, as an Evergreen, with no
words for my love sprouted as needled boughs
and no plan for my knowing

> dropped as seeded cones.

OTHER NAMES

I've notched myself into this steep hillside
above the bustling stream among so many good friends;

the constant companions: Piñon & Cholla, Juniper & Yucca,
Ponderosa, Cottonwood, Willow, as well as those

who summer with us and stand as skeletons all winter
while a new generation is prepared by the workings below:

Blue Grama, Scarlet Gilia, Needle-and-Thread Grass, Wild Aster.
I feel them each slightly grin and lean in as I call their names;

but there's a distance too, a holding back,
something left unsaid, as if I might know them better still.

For the names I use fall flat on the tongue
and squash the breath   they're better left for field guides.

Surely, these leafing ones have other names, richer names,
more akin to their presence, their way upon the land.

I wonder how the ancients addressed these trees—what syllables,
what music—to bring out a broader smile, a closer kinship,

a speaking back, a fluency of conversation. I bet they knelt
and, with a gift, just *asked* these plants for their name instead of

assigning one. And Who is it that whispers our child's name
to us when they're in womb, or sends that music on a dream

for those yearning to hear and follow the all but forgotten way
of deep appellation—calling things just as they are, and can be.

LINEAGE OF SPEECH

Four times the eagle fan tapped my shoulder;
and four times I prayed aloud, my head pressed

firmly against the trunk of the resurrected cottonwood.
Each utterance brought more vigor, and more softness,

to my voice till it was stripped bare of any trace artifice,
and bypassed all cogitating engines to ring like pure

birdcall through the still-wet body of that chosen tree.
Such is the Word as I have known it best, picking me up

like a worn-handled axe to cleave off fresh-cut phrases
that startle life awake in their unguardedness, the medicine

of the moment served to the mouth of Earth
like steaming bread. Four days I danced with brothers

under an endless sun, my face and torso painted, rightly
anointed, in the ancient way. My body fell in a motionless

heap, then—small miracle—it rose to move again:
my feet ever stepping with the drumbeat,

my breath crying through the hollow eagle bone
again & again, my sight bleeding between realms,

my heart pumping on immaterial oil.
Can I utter here that the invisibles appeared?

May I say Earth made us her appointed doctors?
Is it true my tongue spun an enchanted language?

Or mustn't I speak such things? Shall I temper my roar?
I tell you I have spoken thus already in a hundred different

bodies upon a hundred different lands, some whose names
have now turned to wind tones. The space between us is an

open page and upon its clean-washed face, I'll script scraps
of the universe's news in ink that stains and claims completely.

THE INTOXICATOR

When the invisible one who sets my heart to music speaks,
the coded language is always lean and bold:

*Are you fearful of the fall, o blue eyes, of the descent
and the deep, dark passages on a man's rightful path?*

*Will you keep moving in that careful, calculated way,
pre-supposing pitfalls, for another hundred turns of the moon?*

*Do you not yearn for the dead grid of city streets to crumble
apart so you could, for once, be lost and at last present?*

*If I pull you down into the blind matrix of warm clay,
would you dare to sleep a night beside the fiery-haired sun father?*

*And could you dig your way out to air and lay your virgin hands
upon the soft, crystalline underbellies of the star people?*

*Is there not yet something you must do, somewhere you must go,
before you root by the fireplace as the white-bearded storyteller?*

*Or would you rather stay put, all your bookmarks and teacups
in place, your bills and insurances in good order,*
                    rotting from the center outward?

NOBODY

When I invited them, they came, and said:
I'm from generations wide and miles high—
I tunnel like roots—I float like smoke—
I speak from the deeps—My tongue loves
                              the fire and the ice

I boom in as sun spill—I vanish in wisps of shadow—
I loop the sky together as rainbow—
I freefall with raindrops—There's no cloud
                              as fluid-formed as I

So I asked: What of the stones?
We've sat for ages too, sculpted down to bone
                              and then some

Then I inquired: What's in the Earth?
We've pressed our hands on her beating heart
                              singing along

And I implored: Which is the highest dance?
It may be the stars in sleek twirls and long lunges—
Or it might be the dandelion's down
                              in quick shoots and shivers

And I provoked: Which age was most glorious?
The one you know now, the breath you just gave out—
The kingdoms of old and circles of yet hold you here
                              in the fullness and the void—

You are wanderers in wonder, lovers and murderers each—
Shooting up to the fiery heavens,

                                    crumpled down cool in the dirt

REFRESHED

Two days have passed since these lips
stretched to a bite or pursed toward a sip

and hours since any muscle flared;
even my nervous eyelids are unfluttered;

my dutiful thoughts and impassioned
longings have packed up and moved on;

this is just a body at rest.

      am I sprouting roots?
      calcifying to stone?

With no one to look,
the invisibles begin their appearances:

the big bearded one steps out of the mirror;
shimmery wings of an almost-bird fill the window;

a furrish presence squats beside the bed.
There is no message percolating from them,

no murmurings or melodies,
and no feverish swirl of other abortive images.

These three sit still
for as long as my vision beholds them…

And *now* I know them again.
They watched me dance four days;

they heard what I whispered into the loose tobacco;
they rode in on clouds and walked out on sunbeams.

        they've come again to see me!
        can I bear it?

Soon enough, I'll rise, drink and eat
and become busy with tidbits and timing.

But this lying supine on the dark sea bottom encircled
by wondrous creatures could please me for eons:

held firm in these initiatory waters,
denied the breath yet living to the full.

BIG ONE

Only when I was really ready, you seized me,
clenched a fistful of my hair and drew my head close
to breathe your unmincing words down my gullet
like a stinging homebrew; your wild eyes consumed
mine in gulps and cut loose every mooring fastening
me to a smaller-hearted brand of manhood. People
say the ancestors come at times to those with ears
to hear, yet this was my first taste of your voice,
your commanding tongue, your looming presence,
your clear instruction. I sat stunned, listening,
immobile as if upon the surgical table, blades slicing
and brushes sweeping, as the thing I was melted
down and left the original animal of me lying naked
in the glow of an inheritance finally articulated.
You said our people were big, bigger than me.
You said they were hairy too, their cheeks hairier
than mine. You said their feet were often bare and
strutted around big drums. You said they sailed the
ocean thoroughfares with skill and knew the shape
entire of this blue sphere. Then you told me what I
suspected: when I was lost overnight in the depths
of the mountain's frozen gut and danced unceasingly
to survive, you were there with me the whole while.
And then you invited me, venerable ancestor, to call
you by name: *Big One*.
That was the shiniest coin in the trove by far, for

in that a dialogue opened, one I have since wandered
into many times over hoping to know you more.
At the first of the traditional summer dances you
instructed me to offer, some phantom appeared smallish
in the trees on the east side, glaring at me as if to say,
Show me if you're worthy at all. I danced higher then,
my chest risen toward the layered clouds and my feet
spread upon the fiery sand as the shadow watched,
intent and demanding, with only a hint of interest
in this gaunt creature with so far to go before knowing
anything. I danced on, with abandon now, my heart
floating forward unshielded and expanded past
the place of pleasing anything. And then the diminutive
obscure form tucked in the timbers elongated into
a large, big-bearded, fierce-eyed ancient man backlit
by the still early sun, and I knew it must be you.
Your energy softened and issued over the dance circle
like freed water. *Big One*, I whispered dry-mouthed,
*I am your grandson. I want to do something of what you
old ones did. I want to be of use to the Great Mother and
taught by the Great Father. Come to me again.*
And you were gone. And come only at the most
crucial junctures. Knowing the journey is mine
to take. And that I will ride through or drown
in the rough movements of the surrounding seas
as is fitting, or needed. Yet I know there is a secret
tenderness between us and you love to see me
in the wood, shirtless and nimble-footed, flashing
through the trees, growling with the beasts, and taking
pause at the stream to clutch a handful of tobacco and
remember you to the everclear descending waters.

OF MUD AND WOMAN

On the day when seas of women gathered to march
   in every city, pouring through the streets like a new,
speaking water, my soul's twin sat, big-bellied pregnant,
   in a wash of drumming and dreamed her life awake:

She stood nude in a fertile, deep-green, low-lit, wet-dripping
   forest. Her feet felt and drew up an original pulse through
bending knees and circling hips and curling arms and
   an opening mouth that voiced a primal breath sequence,

also pulsing, an animal trance falling upon her like
   rainfall. Her toes splayed into the mud, the squelch of
her steps rising as wet earth splattered up forming a
   warm garment upon her skin while she rocked and spun,

then dropped, rolling in the dark soil, vitals pouring from
   each doorway of the body: blood & urine & milk & feces
& tears & spit all awash in the clay of her dance. And when
   that ancient clay rose and hardened into a first phallus,

she lowered upon it by instinct and knew the ecstasy of joining
   that earth god energy, her breath now sharpening to sound
and a woman scream-song unsung for years rang forth.
   Her belly quickly swelled and rounded and held the girl child

the forest longed for. And on and on she danced until her
   legs opened as lightning shudders of nearly death and stunning

delight jolted through all of her and the baby slid from
    her gaping mound into its place in the mud and the light

and its mother's scooping hands—two earthen bodies molded
    together, swaying slowly down to stillness as silence
blanketed over them and the trees sheltered their slumber.
    When dawn roused her again, she walked, baby-on-chest,

to a low-standing willow lodge covered in fur skins and
    crawled in to sit at the east side. Red-glowing stones were
carried by shadowy forms to a pit in the small room's center
    and water thrown so steam rose and filled the lodge. She

lay head-to-earth, breast-to-child as the mist wound
    round the two and washed them of dried blood and mud
and tears and filled her feminine well with a moist
    medicine that soothed and cooled the wound of birthing.

That healing steam streamed into her mouth too and
    alchemized to milk, the babe lapping furiously at her bosom.
The single mother-child being was held in that earthen
    womb for a full turn of the moon, attended by women who

scuttled in silently with herb-infused waters and baskets of
    flower petals and feather fans and gourd rattles to anoint the
soft, curving body clump daily with oil essences and songs. On
    the appointed morning, they gently brushed out the mother's long,

womanly hair and wove a crown of thirteen feathers into it, then
    dressed both females in blue gowns and motioned to the door where

the forest dwellers all waited to gaze upon their prize. The mother
     emerged and stood upright within a ring of redwoods, and again

danced, the steps now refined in an elegance of one who
     has been expressed and seen and given firm purpose. The baby
grew by the minute, quickly out of cradling arms and standing
     beside her mother, innocently mimicking her steps. The girl was

welcomed into the village life, and as she grew through the
     feminine stages, her mother's hair sprouted silver at the roots
and lengthened till the feather crown dropped below her shoulders.
     She sat then, crone-like, upon the land and received people of all

ages and walks now drawn to her, relishing each syllable she
     spoke or sang among them. And when the girl child was clearly
woman, she too was drawn into the forest to dance the sensuous,
     sinuous lashing in the mud and was likewise entered and given seed,

at which the crone's feathers all fell out and that elder hair
     was white as moonlight. The silver-haired beauty slipped noiselessly
into the trees and found a clearing where the ground was wet and
     ready for her. Her body sank down and down into the sea of clay

until only her head remained above. Her eyes drank deeply, once more,
     of the forest's splendor and her lips released a final breath toward
the watchful trees, and she was consumed by the mouth of earth.
     The girl-become-woman danced on, chin raised to the sun,

babe in arm, and at each footfall, a spiral of mist rose from
     the spot her mother descended; and likewise, breath-like shining
spirals floated throughout the air and sung the continuing
     presence of that mythic woman in tones unheard before or since.

ROUNDING BELLY

Now, later than ever, the air finally begins to cool
and we fall into the fond firm touch of winter's hand,
that way of freeing the growing, breathing things

into long sleeps. And we are here together, my dark-haired
companion, in the shelter of our ongoing dance, the rhythms
renewing so swiftly my feet scramble to keep apace.

Your belly plumps out more each day as a third life
stirs within; knowing, equally, the two waiting outside
and the two who floated silently back to stardust.

And beyond our knowing, we two are stretched into
a larger life. Meanwhile, rising all around us, like mountains,
are insurmountable darknesses that bespeak the mystery

of an age where we seem to love our mothers so feebly.
And the Great Mother claws at her hair, unloved by many
but ever taken by our curiousness, wanting us near yet

prepared to tear us limb-from-limb in the names of all
we cannot reverence. In the midst of this, I am a father
once more and must give thanks, my body becomes a softly

growing song of praise to mirror that invisible sculpting
in your waters. The evergreens affirm my rejoicing
as a necessary balm for the sadness in their needles;

many times I've gone to them and fallen to my knees
in equal parts wonder and despair. Years ago, at a giant
twin-trunked fir, I made a prayer for this girl child now forming.

And this summer past, I drew a circle in the dirt around
one lone pine and fasted there four nights, my body merging
with the humus and drinking from the tap roots, left graciously

undisturbed by miles of moving ants whose work was otherwise.
In honor of the life arriving, I will fast again, befriend the night
and mountainous dark where the ancients breathe. They will

again hear my name and my prayer and make good use of me,
tune me till I am fit to bring my children out each day
to catch the kiss of dawn. Bless you, mother of my heart,

for carrying life in this cold season. My fire will be yours
each night, sprung from tobacco leaves, grown in the wind
of my words, radiating the long narratives entrusted to me.

In spring, we will lay an altar to shepherd you in this birth
and the animal of our common purpose will come through,
naked and hungry in the light, ready to cut a path we cannot

reach or even hope for till, one day, she grips our hands
and drags us out to a meadow that we never imagined
could flower again and lays us down among the wild, colored

blossoms to watch the darkness fall and the stars turn on
like spirit eyes popping open all over the sky, watching us back,
spilling silver upon whatever parenting we managed these years.

THE SICKNESS

Don't get me wrong, I well know the wild places
and presences I love suffer the weight of this

drying, dying time. The wolves are coughing out
blood by moonlight; the gulls are burping up

oil on the shoreline; the evergreens quietly
bleed out the sludge they've drunk and breathed;

and the wildflowers have lost all sense of timing
in their once expert unfurling. I see the eyes

of the clouds burning and feel the Sun boiling
in the rage of a man whose beloved girl cannot be

protected from the merciless continual poisonings
or the still available triggers of big bombs

stockpiled in the soil. The seemingly untouched
forest where I disappear, that pulls me in and

romances me is not a world apart hidden in a private
heaven. It is a sick earth we were born into

and our children will surely inhabit a sicker one still.
But as much as despair is the only tune that tells

it straight, it's also true the old ones knew
what is ours to do and did it, and we must too.

It is no extra-curricular endeavor to move energy
along in song from this green surface world to

the inner clay heart of the Great Mother. It is the main
thing to fashion a prayer and dance it for days, to gather

up scavenged bits of beauty and feed them into the mouth
of a fireplace, to sit with a heart split wide and usher the

liquid medicine of the stars through all of you to the
all of every grieving body of every nuanced species

surrounding you, to visit the forest and lavishly
wash each of your sensory instruments in the icy

fresh streams. In this, you begin to remember who
and how you are and even if you wanted to wallow

in anguish, you'd never have the time,
and, charged by the same flame those ancients

kindled, you could no longer muster the deadness
that before held you captive. Now the privilege of

living in such a critical moment will reckon in you:
either to hold our Mother's hand as she expires,

or to see her rise from one bed of death and walk
outdoors into the rising Sun and dance for him again,

her old soiled garments falling away in his
fiery touch and a new dress opening over her body

like delicate spring blossoms arriving
in wide-eyed innocence after the harshest winter.

ROOT

BACKYARD SANCTUARY

A round hut built of mud and stone and golden
flecks of straw, the honest labor of our hands
coached by mouths murmuring in the soil,
fueled by the colored trill of stars—making a space
to be held holy. And we have held it so, as a family,
even after careless shouting or before a brutal
crossroads, we find ourselves there again together.
And there are nights I enter that earthen womb
alone, while my wife and children slumber,
to spelunk darknesses that men must wrestle
or else die of softness and poverty of magic. I love,
fiercely, this heart of our home and often slip out
the back door just to gaze upon it, standing,
as if for centuries, primitive and perfect, harboring
a fireplace and a water bowl in elegant silence.
Within this curving sanctuary, our son and daughter
were born into bright-colored circles of prayer
and warmth, poems have leapt forth and songs
dropped in, and we've called to the luminous ones
again and again to learn just how to move, what is
ours to do and offer. There we find the courage
to seed and feed all the best leanings of our wild,
dedicated hearts. When the drum beats, when
the rattle shakes, the fire is ignited, the water is
poured out, the air turns sweet with sage smoke;
we breathe as one and anchor in; our minds entrain
with juniper berry and yucca spear; our eyes close

and throats open, sound cascades as fresh medicine;
our feet begin to move like elk, like roadrunner;
and we are there—bouncing, muscle-rippling,
sweaty—awakened in the great dance of it all.

MARRIAGE

When I've forgotten how to *just be*
with you, oh love, I'll go wrap my arms

around an old tree and feel for the slight rise
& fall of its spacious rib cage;

I'll hold hands with a stone
and relish its soft lines and bony textures;

I'll shut these eyes in the pristine sunlight
and allow myself to be gazed upon, fully,

with no veils or visors;
I'll recall once more that we are fleshy first,

that before all our notions bravely orbiting
the future, we are creatures—

hungry and in heat—asleep and at ease—
speaking body-to-body with all the brothers

& sisters of creation (covered in supple down or coarse moss,
dressed in fine-oiled needle gowns or silky many-colored coats)

who each rose, as we did, beauty-struck, from some moist
parting in the soil of this great earthen Body.

And the conversation I enjoy most—may its thread
never finally find an end—

is the one between your body & mine,
even and especially in the long overnight silences

of two hands gently clasped in slumber
under the wool blankets.

ROCKER

I sat on a rocker in the shelter of a wrap-around
front porch at the old-style home, holding our third
and surely final baby asleep on my chest and tasting
into the enormity of this new life so tightly wound to
mine, the flavor of it sharp on my tongue. And a bitter
strain lay there too in the ephemerality, this now angelic
dozing bundle already moving ahead quickly, her
fiercely-here presence suggesting the future absence
all parents find suddenly ringing in their empty cupped
hands. Soft rain fell all around us to finally break the
thick summer heat and mingle with the peaceful
dreamscape of the infant to make a bliss that swelled
my heart to a more fatherly size. In the trees beyond,
a sisterhood of deer appeared, two grown does and
one new-legged fawn, who came to acknowledge
their kin, this child we named 'wild deer dancer' for
she seemingly carried that brand of magic. And indeed
her mother, in receiving her, became possessed of it,
dancing three nights under the moon in a knees-high,
bounding, deer-like beauty I shall ever recall. As I shall
this instant apart, this long draught of ease in the
rocking chair made all the more precious by virtue
of the very hard times. I sat rocking and cataloging the
unearned and never certain comforts of a man's good life:
a healthy baby snoozing on his heart, a home with the
hearth fire ablaze, a light rain feeding the surrounding

rooted ones, four limbs of a familiar female animal
welcoming him in bed to sip the juice of the day's fruits
and refresh the spirit for tomorrow's labor where there
may be a pause—inspired by baby or otherwise—when
the scene goes easy and, without warning, the heart aches
with a strange satisfaction that lingers just long enough
to convince that it's real and its realness can be trusted
even when it vanishes completely and leaves no tracks.

FEVERS

If your gaze is widened and you're in the stream of things,
you'll see it coming. Feel it, really. For days before you'll
casually remark, 'Our little guy is changing', 'Our sweet girl

is getting bigger'. And when the air in the room thickens
with a gravity that wasn't there a moment before, you know
you're in it. Suddenly your child is full of fireworks, bounding

around in furious circles and blasting out the last notes
of a song they've now outgrown. Then the first cough erupts
from your wee one, its gurgles sinister and laced with dark

juices from the belly's deeps. This is the viral figure announcing
himself, spelling out his name and assuring you you will remember
his visit. Instantly, your plans of the next few days all fall away

and a small ceremony begins as your child's little fire flares
into attention and builds for the battle ahead. You frantically
collect necessaries, knowing you will keep vigil all night and tend

that essential flame of the innocent, allowing it to rage just enough
to usher out that dubious initiator who comes, in truth, precisely
when needed and who is unafraid to walk hand-in-hand with your

child's subtle form through the gate whose heat will consume him
even as it uplifts your once-baby becoming more. Over and over
through the night, the brave little body beside you stirs in the bed,

moaning in the ache of this small necessary death. No matter how
routine the illness, the stakes are always high and you sense invisibles
busily circulating the room. These same obscure glows came to oversee

the birth and have come again to insure their favored one will find
her feet once more and continue the music-making she incarnated for.
Yet now the music is replaced with a haunting silence as the old spirit

briefly unfastens from the young body to brave this ritual crossing.
The fire blazes on to its natural peak, then with a reverberating pop
and slow hiss, it finally surrenders its throttle of the lonely body and

the waters break upon the glass-smooth brow of your slight warrior.
And you know the little one has come through the threshold and will,
by daybreak, be off and running, eager as ever, yet carrying a fresh

scar stamped boldly into the pages of their unfolding story. You are
relieved and delighted and more in love than ever with this child
made wholly new in the way that only fire can and surely will again.

OLD FOOL

I scolded my son for calling me a silly old fool—
such brash language at five!—until I realized
he's right. To him, I am. Just as my dad is to me

and all fathers must be for each son to become
possessed of enough gut-wrenching gumption
to leave that first He when the time comes and

cut a road fresh enough to be worth journeying.
With all his might and words, my boy lambasts
my foolishness to go find his place among the

other raucous boys, together building palaces
of their own foolhardiness with the sticks and
mud of their dreamy world. In transgressions

risked and triumphs and collapses shared, they will
learn the smell and shape of brotherhood and seek
it ever as a shelter after long lone voyages and

as a grounding point between easeful passages
among a woman and children. Now I'm an old fool,
but once I too was a boy linked to other boys in

fields of play and on athletic stages. Only by the
boon of a life cleaved off from the broken society
did I eventually find myself in an unbroken circle

of brothers not pitted against other men or ideas
but gathered in a starkly simple unity of purpose:
to dance for Earth. Unheard of in the metropolises

we call cultured, the primeval movement of feet
upon land has settled me beyond all else and dare I
say in this I have begun to engage a brand of

manhood not diluted to convenience or engineered
by the corporate mind. When the bone whistle blows,
an animal know-how awakens in my organism and

brings me into heightened encounter with all animals,
especially the men ringed with me, dry-throated
and open-wounded in the time-tested design of

olden ritual. My son witnesses me thus, and like
any upspringing lad, aspires to one day do as Daddy
does. And perchance he will and become, like me,

an old fool, dancing half-naked around a tree making
gifts to an earth goddess so long neglected her fair skin
went cold and delicate hands clenched shut ages ago.

ARCHETYPES

Every boy, needing adventure, dreams of some
immensity happening through him, the glow of
which will never fully rub off;

Most old men, having adventured, are content
to disappear into the wood and hear the lilt of
their gloried name no more;

What is the territory between?
Who has danced that passage marvelously?

Countless males have leaped into the jaws
of their death-song chasing the feel of that
thunderstruck glow;

Countless others have folded inward
and drowned in the sludge of false burdens
falsely slung upon them;

What is it we cannot know until we've slipped through
the forest's mythic gateway and thus can never tell
our sons, only point the way for them?

Sometimes the darkness ahead and the silence
surrounding are so complete that even a star won't spill
out its glitter, even a bird won't chirp;

If we lit a torch in that deepened dream place,
we'd forget everything shown to us of the world
by many underworldly figures;

Each of us men then must go when called,
without lamp or map, and find our way through
a long, thick wilderness,

at once dazzling and terrifying, and all our own, though,
within it, we are powerfully not alone.

DEAD END

How could we? How could we ever, and in such
short order, squeeze the Earth dry and toss her aside

like a wasted dishrag? How could we so foolishly
fail to fill the myriad tills we emptied or to allow

any rest where we hard-harvested? How could we
recklessly dismiss everything we knew of longevity

and the way all intelligences are tethered together?
How could we employ and never compensate every being

web-knit to us? And how could the old bundles of bones
and seeds and story the elders dutifully handed over

remain unopened for decades? Is this fragile mess
of cluttered buzzing cityscapes all we have left to give

the youth? Will the clutter not soon crumble and the buzz
not one day resoundingly click OFF? Will we become

merely runners from floods and from fires
whose sweep grows swifter and hunger grows grander

till all of this sickly all is swallowed down whole? Will the
bountiful earth garden turn to an irreversibly barren

deadscape, the mountains all headless and the seas each
sludge-slopped? Fortunately, it seems we're not keepers

of much and much of what sustains life occurs in the stars
despite us, their great dust gliding in to tidy things

like an ever-loving mother putting the house back together
while her innocents slumber. All I can do is sing and

sing of the things I love, of breathing many-colored forests
and glistening damp-clouded skies, until my breath runs

out or my heart dries up and cracks to pieces that
will, at least, be sown in the soil that held them so smitten.

COUNTING

I knew the feminine waters had duly
washed through my brain when I stopped
counting and tallying everything—years
of marriage, children's teeth, places
traveled, lovers tasted, times I've died
and let the big soup of this life swirl
and churn unchecked like colliding sea
currents. Then pieces of the past surfaced
readily, not to be accounted for
but chewed on once more, like cud,
and absorbed into the bigger mystery.
All our waifish record-keeping will not
be kept in the earth memory. Every scar
on the body aches to be touched more than
told about, and the child inside will emerge
for play rather than examination. Correlative
to the fall of her waters, the Earth Mother
put a seed of fire in our breasts and will
finally demand to know only how fully it
flamed, and to what immeasurable ends.

GIFTINGS

The vision begins as a
subtle upwelling from the
pit of you, a tiny spurting
that slops over and flows
outward—your fingers lively
with it before your lips. It
was never asked for, nor
could it be. It just arrives
unbidden and then pours
through the body until you
are quite overtaken. You are
bound to a vague image and
a faint sensation that you
cannot exactly recall but
keeps rising into the mind,
tormenting you in the dark with
all that is left undone, all that
was given as yours to become,
if it would only tell you how.

A CUP OF WORDS

When language has been used so much
as a weapon to tear things asunder, to split apart

fabrics so beautifully rendered
and feed the big Pain with more of the same,

       why not go silent for centuries
       and let other musics reclaim the airwaves?

What text is grander than the unfolded page
of a forest: sounded by the wind's promiscuous lips,

printed in sunlight gleaming nude
or clothed in loose clouds?

       But who can hold the tongues of a billion
       anguished bodies with hearts buried prematurely?

When I dug up my own, I found its clay
shaped as a cup. I cannot stop dipping it

into the well of Poetry;
the water is too delicious—

       cool in the mouth, bright in the belly,
       freshness that rises ever stronger

with each cupful passed to friends
in a circle. They drink and are silent.

They walk away and have remembered
how to sing, and why.

TELLING SECRETS

Listen! I will tell you
a secret:

> *the Sun said he loves*
> *the Earth and will go on*
> *loving her further than forever*
> *even if he shuts his eyes*
> *or goes away awhile;*

> *and the Earth told me*
> *we are free,*
> *and filled with purpose,*
> *that we matter much*
> *and alter little*
> *even when we falter big;*

> *and they both winked*
> *& whispered*
> *that one day I might love*
> *someone the way they do each other*
> *and me and all the others.*

That's my secret.
Tell everyone.
(The plants already know.)
(So do the animals.)

AFTERWORD

THE STRANGE MAKING OF AN EARTH POET

As often as I'm able, I take a wander in the wild. And I have learned to count these jaunts among the necessities of life. Recurrently and with unignorable ferocity, I am called away from the demands of domesticity to feel a brief unbridled enchantment among the trees and streams. As a father of three, answering the call is not always easy. Thankfully, my beloved wife grants me allowance to go. In truth, she loves the way I return: wild-eyed, refreshed, inspired, virile!—holding a silver branch or white antler in my hand and a new poem in my mouth.

Each wander is a ritual of sorts and I follow a constantly evolving design that includes writing and reciting poetry as well as making prayers and small observances that delightfully mix my organism with the ecology and the wild allies there living. Each trek is a curious succession of surprises seducing me. Sometimes I am stopped a long while at a particular gnarly root system or clear-sparkled pool. Other times, I am darting along or trudging up to somewhere as yet unknown yet powerfully hungered for. Every time, I have been fed and filled. And I always feed. With foods and herbs and gifts. With present silence and long sitting. With enraptured bushwhacking and primal soundings. And with poems. With heart-bare words spoken to the ears that open in those unspoiled places.

One remarkable time, I walked headlong into a sunny snowstorm, a fairly commonplace happening in the high desert mountains of Santa Fe where I live. A few miles along, the skies darkened and an impenetrable mist swept in suddenly and engulfed me completely. And then—there is no other way to say it—the forest *shifted* and startlingly resembled no place I'd been before. Mystified, I looked left and right repeatedly and simply could not discern where I was or which way to go. I scrambled up as high as I could to find my bearings but, high or low, there was no seeing anything past my hand. The more I clambered up or scurried across or slid down, the more deeply I was pulled into the belly of the canyon until I finally bottomed out at the stream that ran along its long narrow floor. I knew I was nowhere near any human-dug trail, and with daylight dying fast, I was faced with what would surely be a long, dark, cold, and very wet night out. Every stick was iced over and my hands quickly became unfeeling, cumbersome blocks. The only fire to warm me would be the one frightfully sparking in my breast as I sobered to the mounting circumstances. I quickly dug the beginnings of a trench to shelter in, but, upon sitting to test it out, my violently-shaking body told me I must stand and move. Snow turned to sleet and I was soon saturated beyond any hope of drying. Things looked grim. Desperate. Possibly hopeless. Looking back at my partly-dug trench, it now eerily resembled a grave. A choice seemed to present itself: lie down in that hole or find some way to keep my body in motion indefinitely.

Because of a ceremonial background that originated in my early manhood when I served as a schoolteacher on the Pine Ridge Reservation and still continues, I knew I could sing and dance for extended spells. So I sang. And danced. And recited poems. And kept on and on and on. In a way that could only be felt to be known, my body rose into its animal intelligence, revealing and accessing a basic human endurance I never had occasion to feel before. As I shuffled my feet over and over, I came into a state where the spirits of the wild told me things I will never forget, the hints of which speak here and there in this collection. Among the many riches of that night apart was the way my family instinctively tethered themselves to me and survived the ordeal with me. I have lit and tended a sacred fire countless times and developed a powerful kinship with that glowing element. In my experience, you would never go out on the mountain for any serious ritual without a fire being held below. So, when I recognized I had been seized without warning and launched into the biggest ceremony of my life, I felt bereft to be without a fire to anchor me as I journeyed and to reel me back when it was through. Somewhere in the thick of that night, I came to a distinct threshold, my body weary, my spirit fading, and my mind reckoning with the reality that things might go either way. I closed my eyes and asked, as best I knew how, if I was being taken home, being pulled down into the finality of earth.

And then, clear as day, the image of a fire blazing in our wood stove at home appeared, searing red and whipping up on the glass. Not really an image, though. The fire was, somehow, there before me. And instantly I knew my wife must be tending it. For I had indeed lit a fire in the stove that morning for my family to enjoy while I was gone. And wisely, heroically, my wife kept it singing all night, our children lain beside her on animal skins. In so doing, in the old ways of appealing to nature, she enabled my safe return. As I danced on and gazed into the pulsing fire imaged in the clouds above me, I then saw, in sequence, the faces of my wife and children waiting for me. And, from out of the frigid air, beyond anything really explainable, I *felt the fire*. The sort of thing I had only heard of before was extraordinarily occurring as the sensation of tiny heat waves floated toward me and licked at my icy bearded cheek. In the astonishment and unhitched possibility of that moment, a small voice then sounded inside, whispering that this night was not my end, but rather the death of someone I had been and must leave lying in the snow. Scarfing down these words, I was both tenderly comforted and duly challenged, and nearly leapt off the hillside with renewed vigor. And I danced! Not once did I stop or sit throughout the entirety of that endless January night. I couldn't. And when dawn finally did come and the sun—oh glorious fiery Sun!—crested the ridge, I knew the ceremony was complete.

Fortunately, the hearty search & rescue team sent for me stayed true to their mission too. Once the light came and all of us could see more than a few feet ahead, we found each other and they hiked me all the way up to the life waiting for me, my body still vibrating with the sheer resolve pumped through it all night.

I was changed beyond description and, in the days to follow, the changes kept unfolding and deepening. Above all, everything I gazed upon—a tangle-armed juniper, a blue-skinned stone, a cup of clear water, my son's searching eyes—appeared exceptionally vivid, overwhelmingly detailed, and nearly glowing in its *aliveness*. Especially the trees, whose kind I sensed had attentively stood watch and held me in their field through the night, lending me a bit of their fortitude and ease with what is, however difficult. After some weeks, the intensity of this heightened seeing softened, yet the sensibilities remained, scored into me like initiatory scars that would evermore inform my way, my vision, and, profoundly, my language. As I repeatedly fingered the curious contours of those scars, I shudderingly realized the forest's swallowing of me was no accident. It was, in a rather particular way, an answered prayer.

Three years earlier, I had traveled with my young family to Ireland. Among our many adventures, I broke off from my wife and children one day for a very specific pilgrimage to the spring that is the source of the River Boyne. This holy well, one among heaps of ancient sacred sites on that rugged island, was of special interest to me because of its mythic importance as the home of *Bó Fhinn*, the White Cow Goddess, who is the patron of poetry in Irish lore. It is said those who drink of that well's water in June will be made by her into poets. I went to that spot on the thirtieth day of June, found my way to the mound and the well underneath, removed my shoes and shirt and glasses and ritually approached the waters intoning songs and prayers and bearing gifts. Kneeling at the pool's edge, I spoke what could be described as vows into the pristine source waters, words that bound me indelibly to the leanings and hauntings of the altar of poetry. And then I rose and left that place and began a new way of wandering.

Rarely did I dwell on the events of that pilgrimage, but each dawn thereafter, I stood outdoors in prayer and asked the Earth Mother to use me, to possess my bumbling hands and fumbling tongue, and make me her own. And finally, emphatically, in capturing me overnight in the canyon, she did so. On that night of endless dancing in the snow and ice, I was initiated as a poet. Everything before was practice and preparation. And, in a mythic sense, I was married to the mountain that night. Still I go regularly to the wild and many times it is to that same vast canyon that is, in truth, much like a bride: alluring, elegant, complex, dangerous. The best description for what I get up to in those hills is that I attempt, perhaps clumsily, to serve the altar fiercely bestowed to me that fateful night, carrying and employing the dark bundle of what might be called the earth poet. Whenever I'm able, I disappear into the trees and go on the prowl for a new clutch of delightfully strange words that I might sing out, in the wild and in the village. I am at home there in the thick mountains, and my soul belongs. And so long as my sturdy legs will carry me into those hidden places, I'll keep going, convinced that whatever bits I might catch of the luscious songs flitting down the river or the dark stories breathing in the clay, even in translation, the love-drunk hunt is worthy. It is an unreasoned haunting that drives me on and on. For one thing is certain: you do not choose to be an earth poet. The keeper of its clan arrives breathing on the back of your neck in the pitch of night to claim you.

ACKNOWLEDGMENTS

A kiss of deep gratitude to my beloved Madi whose great beauty and free-flowing way both inspired this collection and supported its formation to the utmost. A bow of wholehearted appreciation to my mentors, David Abram and Arkan Lushwala, for their generous ears and careful readings of the poems. A tender word of thanks for Arawaka and for Hilary and Pete Giovale who provided me with residencies in remote settings where the book could be refined, as well as for editor Leslie Browning who expertly midwifed its emergence. A warm embrace for my parents, Christine and John McLaughlin, whose abiding care extends beyond measure. And always, my tearful, wonderstruck praise is given to wild nature and all its presences who openly receive me wander after wander and set my love-drunk tongue to singing.

ABOUT THE AUTHOR

Timothy P. McLaughlin is the editor of the anthology *Walking on Earth & Touching the Sky,* the producer of the album *Moccasins & Microphones,* and the author of the poetry collection *Rooted & Risen.* He is perhaps best known for his powerful style of embodied recitation and storytelling. Raised with Catholicism, he has followed a traditional Lakota spiritual path since early manhood. McLaughlin lives with his wife Madi and their three children in the northern Rio Grande valley beside the Santa Fe mountains where he loves to wander and listen for wild earth poetry.

TimothyPMcLaughlin.com

PRAISING
EARTH

Timothy P. McLaughlin and his wife, Madi Sato, are co-founders of
PRAISING EARTH, an organization that works to re-root oral
traditions in modern culture as a means of enlivening all peoples' essential
belonging to Earth. PRAISING EARTH houses a variety of offerings,
including women's and men's circles and retreats, immersion programs
in the way of the song carrier and the rewilded human, community
celebrations of song, prayer, and dance, and a wisdom-keepers alliance.
All projects and initiatives are done in community and with consultation
from elders.

PraisingEarth.org

HOMEBOUND PUBLICATIONS
POETRY OFFERINGS

———

HOMEBOUND PUBLICATIONS

Ensuring that the mainstream isn't the only stream.

AT HOMEBOUND PUBLICATIONS, we publish books written by independent voices for independent minds. Our books focus on a return to simplicity and balance, connection to the earth and each other, and the search for meaning and authenticity. We strive to ensure that the mainstream is not the only stream. In all our titles, our intention is to introduce new perspectives that will directly aid humankind in the trials we face at present as a global village.

WWW.HOMEBOUNDPUBLICATIONS.COM
LOOK FOR OUR TITLES WHEREVER BOOKS ARE SOLD

SINCE 2011